بِسْمِ ٱللهِ ٱلرَّحْمَـٰنِ ٱلرَّحِيمِ

Assalamu Alaykum wa Rahmat Allah wa Barakatuh,

Dear Reader,

One of the best acts of worship in Islam is reciting the Quran beautifully and smoothly.

The Prophet (Salla Allahu Alaihi wa Sallam) said:

"Verily the one who recites the Qur'an beautifully, smoothly, and precisely, he will be in the company of the noble and obedient angels. And as for the one who recites with difficulty, stammering or stumbling through its verses, then he will have TWICE that reward." [Al-Bukhari and Muslim]

Ever since teaching Quran to non Arabic speaking students, I realised the need to write a manual which would equip the students to recite the holy Quran beautifully and smoothly.

Janat Al Quran books aim to make learning the Quran easy for all students whether adults or children, beginners or advanced level. The books explain the Tajweed rules in English while the terms remain in Arabic with a translation for each term.

The books explain the Tajweed rules according to the narration of Hafs from the Imam Asem in the way of Ash-Shaatibiyah.

My sincere thanks go to my teachers who have taught me the science of Tajweed and the Quran recitation in the ten Qira'at. Special thanks to my sisters in Islam who helped me to enhance the books.

Message to the students:
Learning the Quran with a qualified teacher is of paramount importance. Correct recitation of the Quran can only be achieved through regular practice of the Quran with a teacher who can correct the mistakes.

Reciting the Quran on a daily basis is essential so the student can correct the mistakes pointed out by the teacher. Regular duas and patience are important to make your Quran journey easy and full of Barakah.

Message to the teachers:
Kindly be reminded to always renew your intention for teaching the Quran and to ensure the work is done solely for Allah's sake. It is important that we always motivate the students and inspire them to love the Quran.

May Allah Subhanahu wa Ta'la accept all our good deeds to please Him. May Allah unite us all in Jannah with his prophet Salla Allahu Alaihi wa Sallam.

Dina Essam

What some Shaykhs and teachers have said about the book

The Quran is the word of Allah which was revealed to the heart of the prophet SAW with an Arabic tongue. It was revealed Muratal (recited beautifully with Tajweed), that is the way it should always be recited and listened to so the listener can be in the beautiful Jannah of the Quran.

Jannat Al Quran books is a fantastic attempt from Shaykha Dina to get the reciter reach the Jannah of the Quran in order to make the Quran a path to the Firdaws in the hereafter in Shaa Allah. The Tajweed rules are explained with simplicity and clarity for anyone to understand. May Allah SWT reward the author of the book and the learners of the Quran.

Shaykh Samir Abd-Alazeem
Al-Azhar University

I would like to thank Shaykha Dina Essam for this great effort. We have always acknowledged this Khair and hard work from her in serving Allah's religion and His holy book.

I have read Jannat Al Quran books and found a good organisation for all the books and an easy explanation for all the Tajweed rules. Having all the Tajweed rules in those set of books makes the reader or the knowledge seeker who has learned the rules able to recite the Quran precisely with Allah's will. May Allah grant you success.

Shaykh Tamer Ibrahim,
Al-Azhar University

What some Shaykhs and teachers have said about the book

In the name of Allah who has revealed the holy book. I ask Allah to grant success to everyone who serves His religion, and give Barakah to Janat Al Quran books, this great work, that serves Allah's book.

These books give the chance to non Arabic speakers to understand the science of Tajweed of His book, for what they contain of valuable knowledge and simple method of explanation.

Sincere thanks to those who have helped in getting this book to the light in this way that is suitable for serving Allah's book.

I ask Allah to grant success to the writer and the learners of these books. May Allah grant Hidayah (guidance) to people through the learners of His book and may they become the best of people as the prophet said, "The best among you are those who learn the Qur'an and teach it.".

Mostafa Ibrahim
Al-Azhar University

The structure of Jannat Al Quran books will allow the student to successfully study the highly complex science of tajweed with simplicity. I would recommend it for sure!

Ayah Yussuf Teama
Al-Azhar University

Table of Contents

First Section

Hamza-tul Qata' (ء) & Hamza-tul Wasl (أ)

Jannat
Al Quran

Hamza-tul Qata' (ء)
& Hamza-tul Wasl (ٱ)

There are two types of Hamzah in the Quran. They have different forms and rules.

A) Hamza-tul Qata' (ء)

Definition:
The letter Hamzah appears in many different forms in the Arabic language, but it is pronounced according to the Harakah above or below the Hamzah.

Examples:

إ - أ - ئ - ؤ - ء

Hamza-tul Qata' can either be at the beginning, or in the middle, or at the end of a word.

Examples:

ءَأَنْتُم - أَحْمَد - سَأَلَ - مُؤْمِنَة - بَرِىءٌ - بِئْسَ - سَمَاءٌ

Note:
The Alif and Hamzah are 2 different letters. For Uthmani script, the letter Alif will never have Harakah whilst for Indo Pak script, the letter Alif may have Harakahs. In the latter case, the Alif is pronounced as Hamzah.

Hamza-tul Qata' (ء)
& Hamza-tul Wasl (ٱ)

A) Hamza-tul Qata' (ء)

Common Mistakes:

1- Not pronouncing the همزة clearly when it is repeated.

Examples: ءَأَنتَ — ءَإِنَّكَ

2- Not pronouncing the عين from the right point of articulation when preceded by همزة.

Examples: أَعُوذُ — أَعْلَمُ

3- همزة should be pronounced clearly when it is Saakin otherwise it will be pronounced as the letters of Madd.

Examples: مُؤْصَدَةٌ - شِئْتُمْ - فَأْتُوا

B) Hamza-tul Wasl (ٱ)

Definition: Hamzah-tul Wasl is pronounced when starting the words, and dropped when continuing.

Hamzah-tul Wasl appears only at the beginning of a word. It has a little saad written on top of Alif (صـ). If the reciter starts reciting from a word that begins with Hamza-tul Wasl, then it should be pronounced with Harakah. However, it is not pronounced when joining the word that starts with Hamzah-tul Wasl with the previous word.

Hamzah-tul Wasl can be pronounced with i) Fathah, ii) Kasrah or iii) Dhammah according to the following letter.

Hamza-tul Qata' (ء)
& Hamza-tul Wasl (ٱ)

B) Hamza-tul Wasl (ٱ)

i) It is pronounced with a Fathah when it is at the beginning of a noun and is followed by Laam Shamseeyah or Laam Qamareeyah.

Examples:

ٱلْحَمْدُ لِلَّهِ رَبِّ ٱلْعَالَمِين سُورَةُ ٱلْفَاتِحَة الآية ٢

ii) It is pronounced with a Kasrah when it is at the beginning of a verb and the third letter of the verb has a Fathah or a Kasrah.

Examples:

إِلَّا إِبْلِيسَ ٱسْتَكْبَرَ وَكَانَ مِنْ ٱلْكَافِرِينَ سُورَةُ ص الآية ٧٤

ٱسْتَغْفِرْ لَهُمْ أَوْ لَا تَسْتَغْفِرْ لَهُمْ سُورَةُ ٱلتَّوْبَة الآية ٨٠

It is also pronounced with a Kasrah in seven nouns in the Quran. For example:

1- وَنَادَى نُوحٌ رَّبَّهُ فَقَالَ رَبِّ إِنَّ ٱبْنِي مِنْ أَهْلِي وَإِنَّ وَعْدَكَ ٱلْحَقُّ وَأَنْتَ أَحْكَمُ ٱلْحَاكِمِينَ سُورَةُ هُود الآية ٤٥

2- وَمَرْيَمَ ٱبْنَتَ عِمْرَانَ ٱلَّتِي أَحْصَنَتْ فَرْجَهَا سُورَةُ ٱلتَّحْرِيم الآية ١٢

3

Hamza-tul Qata' (ء)
& Hamza-tul Wasl (ٱ)

B) Hamza-tul Wasl (ٱ)

3- إِنِ ٱمْرُؤٌ هَلَكَ سُورَةُ النِّسَاء الآية ﴿١٧٦﴾

4- وَإِنِ ٱمْرَأَةٌ خَافَتْ مِنْ بَعْلِهَا نُشُوزًا أَوْ إِعْرَاضًا فَلَا جُنَاحَ عَلَيْهِمَا أَنْ

يُصْلِحَا بَيْنَهُمَا صُلْحًا وَالصُّلْحُ خَيْرٌ سُورَةُ النِّسَاء الآية ﴿١٢٨﴾

5- وَقَالَ اللَّهُ لَا تَتَّخِذُوا إِلَهَيْنِ ٱثْنَيْنِ إِنَّمَا هُوَ إِلَهٌ وَاحِدٌ فَإِيَّايَ فَارْهَبُونِ

سُورَةُ النَّحْل الآية ﴿٥١﴾

6- نِسَاءً فَوْقَ ٱثْنَتَيْنِ سُورَةُ النِّسَاء الآية ﴿١١﴾

7- سَبِّحْ ٱسْمَ رَبِّكَ الْأَعْلَى سُورَةُ الْأَعْلَى الآية ﴿١﴾

iii) It is pronounced with a Dhammah when it is at the beginning of a verb and the third letter of the verb has a Dhammah.

Examples:

فَمَنِ ٱضْطُرَّ غَيْرَ بَاغٍ وَلَا عَادٍ فَلَا إِثْمَ عَلَيْهِ إِنَّ اللَّهَ غَفُورٌ رَحِيمٌ

سُورَةُ الْبَقَرَة الآية ﴿١٧٣﴾

ٱدْعُ إِلَى سَبِيلِ رَبِّكَ بِالْحِكْمَةِ وَالْمَوْعِظَةِ الْحَسَنَةِ

سُورَةُ النَّحْل الآية ﴿١٢٥﴾

Hamza-tul Qata' (ء)
& Hamza-tul Wasl (أ)

B) Hamza-tul Wasl (أ)

Exception:

The following 5 verbs in the Quran are pronounced with Kasrah. Although the third letter has a Dhammah but the reciter starts with a Kasrah as the Dhammah is not part of the original verb due to grammatical rules:

١- ثُمَّ اقْضُوا إِلَيَّ وَلَا تُنظِرُونِ

سُورَةُ يُونُس الآيَة ⑦١

٢- فَقَالُوا ابْنُوا عَلَيْهِم بُنْيَـٰنًا رَّبُّهُم أَعْلَمُ بِهِم

سُورَةُ الكَهْف الآيَة ②١

٣- وَامْضُوا حَيْثُ تُؤْمَرُونَ

سُورَةُ الحِجْر الآيَة ⑥٥

٤- وَانطَلَقَ الْمَلَأُ مِنْهُم أَنِ امْشُوا وَاصْبِرُوا عَلَىٰ ءَالِهَتِكُمْ

سُورَةُ ص الآيَة ⑥

٥- فَأَجْمِعُوا كَيْدَكُم ثُمَّ ائْتُوا صَفًّا

سُورَةُ طه الآيَة ⑥٤

5

Hamza-tul Qata' (ء)
& Hamza-tul Wasl (ٱ)

The differences between Hamza-tul Wasl and Hamza-tul Qata' are noted in the following table:

Hamza-tul Qata'	Hamza-tul Wasl
It can either be at the beginning, or in the middle, or at the end of a word.	It appears only at the beginning of a word.
It is always pronounced, whether the reciter starts by reciting from a word that begins with Hamza-tul Qata' or joins it to the previous word.	It is pronounced if the reciter starts reciting from a word that begins with Hamza-tul Wasl. It is, however, not pronounced when joining the word that starts with Hamzah-tul Wasl with the previous word.
It can have a Harakah or a Sukoon. Its pronunciation doesn't depend on the following letter.	It has no Harakah on top of it and is pronounced with a Fathah or a Kasrah or a Dhammah, according to the following letter.
It appears in different forms.	It has only one form.

The Meeting of Hamza-tul Wasl and Hamza-tul Qata' in One Word

There are two ways that this occurs:

a) Hamza-tul Wasl precedes the Hamza-tul Qata'

b) Hamza Qata' precedes the Hamza-tul Wasl (questioning Hamza)(1)

A) Hamza-tul Wasl Precedes a Hamza-tul Qata' which is Saakinah

Examples:

1– فَإِنْ أَمِنَ بَعْضُكُم بَعْضًا فَلْيُؤَدِّ ٱلَّذِى ٱؤْتُمِنَ أَمَـٰنَتَهُۥ وَلْيَتَّقِ ٱللَّهَ

رَبَّهُۥ ۗ سورة البَقَرَة الآية ﴿٢٨٣﴾

2– وَقَالُواْ يَـٰصَـٰلِحُ ٱئْتِنَا بِمَا تَعِدُنَآ إِن كُنتَ مِنَ ٱلْمُرْسَلِينَ

سورة الْأَعْرَاف الآية ﴿٧٧﴾

3– وَمِنْهُم مَّن يَقُولُ ٱئْذَن لِّى وَلَا تَفْتِنِّىٓ ۚ سورة التَّوْبَة الآية ﴿٤٩﴾

4– فَأَجْمِعُواْ كَيْدَكُمْ ثُمَّ ٱئْتُواْ صَفًّا ۚ سورة طه الآية ﴿٦٤﴾

5– ٱئْتُونِى بِكِتَـٰبٍ مِّن قَبْلِ هَـٰذَا سورة الْأَحْقَاف الآية ﴿٤﴾

There are two rulings:

1- Hamza-tul wasl is not pronounced when the word starting with it is joined to the preceding word.

Note (1): A Questioning Hamzah is a Hamzah which turns a statement to a question.

7

The Meeting of Hamza-tul Wasl and Hamza-tul Qata' in One Word

2- If the reciter starts reciting the word that has Hamza-tul wasl, it is pronounced with Harakah according to the following letter, Hamza-tul Qata' is changed to a letter of Madd according to the Harakah of Hamza-tul wasl.

The following words will show how the previous examples are pronounced when the reciter starts reading these words:

1- أُوتُمِنَ

2- إِيتِنَا

3- إِيذَن

4- إِيتُواْ

5- إِيتُونِي

B) Hamza-tul Qata' Precedes Hamza-tul Wasl (Questioning Hamzah).

Hamza-tul Wasl will have two rulings in three nouns that occur in the Quran:

1- Hamza-tul Wasl will change to an Alif Madd and will be prolonged 6 Harakas as it is followed by a Saakin letter.

2- Tasheel will be done on Hamza-tul Wasl. Tasheel means pronouncing Hamza-tul Wasl as a sound which is neither Hamza nor Alif Madd, but a sound in between. No elongation will be done.

The Meeting of Hamza-tul Wasl and Hamza-tul Qata' in One Word

All the words are mentioned in the Quran:

قُلْ ءَآللَّهُ أَذِنَ لَكُمْ سُورَةُ يُونُس الآية ٥٩

ءَآللَّهُ خَيْرٌ أَمَّا يُشْرِكُونَ سُورَةُ النَّمْل الآية ٥٩

ءَآلْـَٰنَ وَقَدْ كُنتُم بِهِۦ تَسْتَعْجِلُونَ سُورَةُ يُونُس الآية ٥١

ءَآلْـَٰنَ وَقَدْ عَصَيْتَ قَبْلُ وَكُنتَ مِنَ ٱلْمُفْسِدِينَ سُورَةُ يُونُس الآية ٩١

قُلْ ءَآلذَّكَرَيْنِ حَرَّمَ أَمِ ٱلْأُنثَيَيْنِ سُورَةُ الْأَنْعَام الآية ١٤٣،١٤٤

Notes:

The word ٱلْأَيْكَةِ occurs four times in the Quran.

i) It occurs twice with Hamza-tul Wasl in the following Ayahs:

1- وَإِن كَانَ أَصْحَٰبُ ٱلْأَيْكَةِ لَظَٰلِمِينَ سُورَةُ الْحِجْر الآية ٧٨

2- وَأَصْحَٰبُ ٱلْأَيْكَةِ وَقَوْمُ تُبَّعٍ سُورَةِ ق الآية ١٤

9

The Meeting of Hamza-tul Wasl and Hamza-tul Qata' in One Word

Hamza-tul Wasl will be pronounced with Fathah when the reciter begins reading these words without joining with the previous words.

ii) It occurs twice without Hamza-tul Wasl in the following Ayahs:

1- كَذَّبَ أَصْحَٰبُ لْئَيْكَةِ ٱلْمُرْسَلِينَ سُورَةُ الشُّعَرَاءِ الآية ﴿١٧٦﴾

2- وَثَمُودُ وَقَوْمُ لُوطٍ وَأَصْحَٰبُ لْئَيْكَةِ سُورَةُ ص الآية ﴿١٣﴾

Hamza-tul Wasl will be added to the above examples and pronounced with a Fathah when the reciter begins reading these words without joining with the previous words.

The word ٱلِٱسْم that occurs in Surah Al-Hujurat has two pronunciations when the reciter starts by this word.

بِئْسَ ٱلِٱسْمُ ٱلْفُسُوقُ بَعْدَ ٱلْإِيمَٰنِ سُورَةُ الحُجُرَات الآية ﴿١١﴾

1- Hamza-tul Wasl is pronounced with a Fathah and that is the preference.
It will be pronounced as follows: أَلِٱسْم

2- Hamza-tul Wasl is dropped and the Laam is pronounced with a Kasrah. It will be pronounced as follows: لِٱسْم

Exercises

1- What are the differences between Hamza-tul Wasl and Hamza-tul Qata'?

2- Complete the following:
a) Hamza-tul Wasl is pronounced with .... when it is at the beginning of a noun and is followed by Laam Shamseeyah and Laam Qamareeyah.
b) Hamza-tul Wasl is pronounced with .... when it is at the beginning of a verb and the third letter of the verb has a Fathah or a Kasrah.
c) Hamza-tul Wasl is pronounced with .... when it is at the beginning of a verb and the third letter of the verb has a Dhammah.

3- How should the reciter begin his recitation from the words written in red below:

a) وَمَرْيَمَ ٱبْنَتَ عِمْرَانَ ٱلَّتِي أَحْصَنَتْ فَرْجَهَا

b) ٱدْعُ إِلَىٰ سَبِيلِ رَبِّكَ بِٱلْحِكْمَةِ وَٱلْمَوْعِظَةِ ٱلْحَسَنَةِ

c) فَأَجْمِعُوا۟ كَيْدَكُمْ ثُمَّ ٱئْتُوا۟ صَفًّا

d) ٱئْتُونِي بِكِتَٰبٍ مِّن قَبْلِ هَٰذَا

e) قُلْ ءَآللَّهُ أَذِنَ لَكُمْ

f) كَذَّبَ أَصْحَٰبُ لْئَيْكَةِ ٱلْمُرْسَلِينَ

g) وَأَصْحَٰبُ ٱلْأَيْكَةِ وَقَوْمُ تُبَّعٍ

Second Section

Relationships
Between Letters

Jannat
Al Quran

Relationships Between Letters

There are four types of relationships between letters:

A) Likeness تَمَاثُل

B) Similarity تَجَانُس

C) Closeness تَقَارُب

D) Distant تَبَاعُد

A) The Relationship of Likeness - التَّمَاثُل

Definition: It is the relationship between two letters that share the same point of articulation and characteristics (sifaat), in other words, the two letters are identical.

There are three types of Likeness

i) The small likeness الْمُتَمَاثِلَان الصَّغِير

ii) The great likeness الْمُتَمَاثِلَان الْكَبِير

iii) The mutlaq likeness الْمُتَمَاثِلَان الْمُطْلَق

i) The Small Likeness الْمُتَمَاثِلَان الصَّغِير

Definition: It is when the two identical letters are next to each other. The first letter has Sukoon and the second one has Harakah.

Ruling: Idghaam - the two letters will be merged together to become a Mushaddad letter.

It will be called:

إِدْغَام مُتَمَاثِلَيْنِ صَغِير

It is called small الصَّغِير as the first letter has Sukoon and the second one has Harakah; therefore, it is easy to make Idghaam.

Examples:

أَنِ اضْرِب بِّعَصَاكَ ٱلْحَجَرَ ۖ سُورَةُ الْأَعْرَاف الآية ﴿١٦٠﴾

وَقَد دَّخَلُواْ بِٱلْكُفْرِ وَهُمْ قَدْ خَرَجُواْ بِهِ ۚ سُورَةُ الْمَائِدَة الآية ﴿٦١﴾

فَقَدْ جَعَلْنَا لِوَلِيِّهِۦ سُلْطَٰنًا فَلَا يُسْرِف فِّي ٱلْقَتْلِ ۖ سُورَةُ الْإِسْرَاء الآية ﴿٣٣﴾

أَيْنَمَا تَكُونُواْ يُدْرِككُّمُ ٱلْمَوْتُ وَلَوْ كُنتُمْ فِي بُرُوجٍ مُّشَيَّدَةٍ

سُورَةُ النِّسَاء الآية ﴿٧٨﴾

وَيَجْعَل لَّكَ قُصُورًا سُورَةُ الْفُرْقَان الآية ﴿١٠﴾

ذَٰلِكَ بِمَا عَصَوا۟ وَّكَانُواْ يَعْتَدُونَ سُورَةُ الْبَقَرَة الآية ﴿٦١﴾

Exceptions:

When the Waaw Madd precedes the letter Waaw, and the Yaa Madd precedes the letter Yaa. There will be no Idghaam, as the Makhraj of the Madd letters is the Jawf, which is not the same as that of the next letter. This Madd is called Madd Tamkeen مَدُّ التَّمْكِين

Examples:

ٱلَّذِى يُوَسْوِسُ فِى صُدُورِ ٱلنَّاسِ سُورَةُ النَّاس الآية ﴿٥﴾

إِنَّ ٱلَّذِينَ ءَامَنُواْ وَعَمِلُواْ ٱلصَّٰلِحَٰتِ أُوْلَٰٓئِكَ هُمْ خَيْرُ ٱلْبَرِيَّةِ

سُورَةُ الْبَيِّنَة الآية ﴿٧﴾

Note: If the first letter is Waaw Leen, the ruling of Idghaam applies.

ذَٰلِكَ بِمَا عَصَوا۟ وَّكَانُواْ يَعْتَدُونَ

Relationships Between Letters

ii) The Great Likeness الْمُتَمَاثِلَانِ الْكَبِير

Definition: It is when two identical letters are next to each other and both have Harakahs.

Ruling: Izhaar, except in a few words in the Quran.

It is called the great likeness (الْكَبِير) as both letters have Harakahs. In case of Idghaam, the Harakah of the first letter has changed to be Sukoon, then the first letter has been merged into the next one.

Examples of Izhaar:

الرَّحْمَـٰنِ الرَّحِيمِ   مَـٰلِكِ يَوْمِ الدِّينِ   سُورَةُ الفَاتِحَة الآية ﴿١﴾ ﴿٣﴾

ذَٰلِكَ الْكِتَـٰبُ لَا رَيْبَ فِيهِ هُدًى لِّلْمُتَّقِينَ   سُورَةُ البَقَرَة الآية ﴿٢﴾

مَا سَلَكَكُمْ فِي سَقَرَ   سُورَةُ المُدَّثِّر الآية ﴿٤٢﴾

Exceptions:

A few words occur in the Quran where the ruling of Idghaam, instead of Izhaar, is applied.

This is called إِدْغَام مُتَمَاثِلَيْنِ كَبِير

Examples:

قَالَ مَا مَكَّنِّي فِيهِ رَبِّي خَيْرٌ   سُورَةُ الكَهْف الآية ﴿٩٥﴾ (1

The original word is مَكَّنَنِي. The first Noon has Fathah, which has been changed to Sukoon and merged into the next Noon. Therefore, the Noon is pronounced with Shaddah.

Relationships Between Letters

قَالُواْ يَـٰٓأَبَانَا مَالَكَ لَا تَأۡمَنَّا عَلَىٰ يُوسُفَ وَإِنَّا لَهُ ۥ لَنَـٰصِحُونَ (2)

سُورَةُ يُوسُف الآية⑪

The original word is تَأۡمَنُنَا. The first Noon has Dhammah, which has been changed to Sukoon and merged into the next Noon. Therefore, the Noon is pronounced with Shaddah.

This word can be pronounced in two ways:

a. Idghaam and Ishmam إِشۡمَام - making the sign of Dhammah (rounding the lips) when pronouncing the first Saakin Noon without making the actual sound of Dhammah. Therefore, it is just a sign without sound.

b. Rawm - pronouncing part of the first Dhammah of the Noon. This means the reciter only gives the Dhammah one-third of its full timing.

iii) The Mutlaq Likeness الْمُتَمَاثِلَانِ الْمُطۡلَق

Definition: It is when the two identical letters are next to each other. The first letter has Harakah and the second one has Sukoon.

Ruling: Izhaar

It is called Mutlaq الْمُطۡلَق as it is neither small nor great.

Examples:

تُتۡلَى - شَقَقۡنَا - فَرَرۡتُمۡ

15

Relationships Between Letters

B) The Relationship of Similarity - التَّجَانُس

Definition: It is the relationship between two letters that share the same point of articulation but different characteristics (Sifaat).

There are three types of similarity:
j) The small similarity المُتَجَانِسَان الصَّغِير
ii) The great similarity المُتَجَانِسَان الكَبِير
iii) The Mutlaq similarity المُتَجَانِسَان المُطْلَق

i) The Small Similarity المُتَجَانِسَان الصَّغِير

Definition: It is when two letters that share the same point of articulation but different Sifaat are next to each other. The first letter has Sukoon and the second one has Harakah.

Ruling: These two letters will merge together (Idghaam) to become one Mushaddad letter. This occurs when letters in the following table meet together.

It will be called: إِدْغَام مُتَجَانِسَيْنِ صَغِير

It is called small الصَّغِير as the first letter has Sukoon and the second one has Harakah; therefore, it is easy to make Idghaam.

Relationships Between Letters

The letters	Examples	The Ruling
باء - ميم	يَـٰبُنَىَّ ٱرْكَب مَّعَنَا وَلَا تَكُن مَّعَ ٱلْكَـٰفِرِينَ سُورَةُ هُود الآية ⟨٤٢⟩	Complete Idghaam
ميم - باء	تَرْمِيهِم بِحِجَارَةٍ مِّن سِجِّيلٍ سُورَةُ الفِيل الآية ⟨٤⟩	Ikhfaa Shafawi
تاء - دال	فَلَمَّآ أَثْقَلَت دَّعَوَا ٱللَّهَ رَبَّهُمَا سُورَةُ الأَعْرَاف الآية ⟨١٨٩⟩ قَالَ قَدْ أُجِيبَت دَّعْوَتُكُمَا سُورَةُ يُونُس الآية ⟨٨٩⟩	Complete Idghaam
دال - تاء	قَد تَّبَيَّنَ ٱلرُّشْدُ مِنَ ٱلْغَيِّ سُورَةُ البَقَرَة الآية ⟨٢٥٦⟩ إِلَّا ٱلَّذِينَ عَـٰهَدتُّمْ عِندَ ٱلْمَسْجِدِ ٱلْحَرَامِ سُورَةُ التَّوْبَة الآية ⟨٧⟩ قَالَ تَٱللَّهِ إِن كِدتَّ لَتُرْدِينِ سُورَةُ الصَّافَات الآية ⟨٥٦⟩	Complete Idghaam
تاء - طاء	إِذ هَمَّت طَّآئِفَتَانِ مِنكُمْ أَن تَفْشَلَا وَٱللَّهُ وَلِيُّهُمَا سُورَةُ آل عِمرَان الآية ⟨١٢٢⟩ فَـَٔامَنَت طَّآئِفَةٌ مِّن بَنِىٓ إِسْرَآءِيلَ وَكَفَرَت طَّآئِفَةٌ سُورَةُ الصَّف الآية ⟨١٤⟩	Complete Idghaam

17

Relationships Between Letters

The letters	Examples	The Ruling
طاء - تاء	لَئِن بَسَطتَ إِلَيَّ يَدَكَ لِتَقْتُلَنِى سُورَةُ الْمَائِدَةِ الآيَةِ ۲۸ فَمَكَثَ غَيْرَ بَعِيدٍ فَقَالَ أَحَطتُ بِمَا لَمْ تُحِطْ بِهِ سُورَةُ النَّمْلِ الآيَةِ ۲۲ أَن تَقُولَ نَفْسٌ يَـٰحَسْرَتَىٰ عَلَىٰ مَا فَرَّطتُ فِى جَنبِ اللَّهِ سُورَةُ الزُّمَرِ الآيَةِ ٥٦	Incomplete Idghaam تاء is stronger than طاء so the heaviness of طاء is kept.
ذال - ظاء	وَلَوْ أَنَّهُمْ إِذ ظَّلَمُوٓاْ أَنفُسَهُمْ جَآءُوكَ فَٱسْتَغْفَرُواْ ٱللَّهَ سُورَةُ النِّسَاءِ الآيَةِ ٦٤ وَلَن يَنفَعَكُمُ ٱلْيَوْمَ إِذ ظَّلَمْتُمْ أَنَّكُمْ فِى ٱلْعَذَابِ مُشْتَرِكُونَ سُورَةُ الزُّخْرُفِ الآيَةِ ٣٩	Complete Idghaam
ثاء - ذال	فَمَثَلُهُۥ كَمَثَلِ ٱلْكَلْبِ إِن تَحْمِلْ عَلَيْهِ يَلْهَثْ أَوْ تَتْرُكْهُ يَلْهَث ذَّٰلِكَ مَثَلُ ٱلْقَوْمِ ٱلَّذِينَ كَذَّبُواْ بِـَٔايَـٰتِنَا سُورَةُ الْأَعْرَافِ الآيَةِ ١٧٦	Complete Idghaam

Relationships Between Letters

ii) The Great Similarity الْمُتَجَانِسَانِ الْكَبِير

Definition: It is when two letters that share the same point of articulation but different Sifaat meet next to each other. Both of them are vowelled.

Ruling: Izhaar

It is called great الْكَبِير as both letters have Harakah.

Examples: الصَّالِحَاتِ طُوبَى - شَجَرَة - بِمَا

iii) The Mutlaq Similarity الْمُتَجَانِسَانِ الْمُطْلَق

Definition: It is when two letters that share the same point of articulation but different Sifaat meet next to each other. The first letter has Harakah and the second one has Sukoon.

Ruling: Izhaar

It is called الْمُطْلَق as it is neither small nor great.

Examples: أَفَتَطْمَعُونَ - يَشْكُرُونَ - أَهْوَاءَهُمْ

Relationships Between Letters

C) The Relationship of Closeness التَّقَارُب

Definition: It is when the two letters, close in the points of articulation and the Sifaat, are situated next to each other. The scholars classified the letters to three categories as follows:

1- Two letters that are close in the points of articulation and Sifaat:

a) The Small Closeness الْمُتَقَارِبَانِ الصَّغِير

Definition: It is when the two letters, close in the points of articulation and the Sifaat, are situated next to each other. The first letter has Sukoon and the second has Harakah.

Examples: الثاء & التاء - النون & اللام

كَذَّبَتْ ثَـمُودُ – مِن لَّدُنْهُ

b) The Great Closeness الْمُتَقَارِبَانِ الْكَبِير

Definition: It is when the two letters, close in the points of articulation and the Sifaat, situate next to each other. Both of them have Harakas.

Examples: الكاف & القاف

مِن فَوْقِكُمْ

Relationships Between Letters

c) The Mutlaq Closeness الْمُتَقَارِبَانِ الْمُطْلَق

Definition: It is when the two letters, close in the points of articulation and the Sifaat, situate next to each other. The first letter has Harakah and the second one has Sukoon.

Examples: الثاء & التاء

وَلَا يَسْتَثْنُونَ

2- Two letters that are close in the points of articulation but not in the Sifaat.

a) The Small Closeness الْمُتَقَارِبَانِ الْصَغِير

Definition: It is when the two letters, close in the points of articulation but not in the Sifaat, situate next to each other. The first letter has Sukoon and the second one has Harakah.

Examples: الدال & السين

قَدْ سَمِعَ

b) The Great Closeness الْمُتَقَارِبَانِ الْكَبِير

Definition: It is when the two letters, close in the points of articulation but not in the Sifaat, situate next to each other. Both of them have Harakas.

Examples: الدال & السين

عَدَدَ سِنِينَ

Relationships Between Letters

c) The Mutlaq Closeness الْمُتَقَارِبَانِ الْمُطْلَق

Definition: It is when the two letters, close in the points of articulation but not in the Sifaat, situate next to each other. The first letter has Harakah and the second one has Sukoon.

Examples: السين & النون

سُندُسٍ

3- Two letters that are close in the Sifaat but not in the points of articulation.

a) The Small Closeness الْمُتَقَارِبَانِ الصَغِير

Definition: It is when the two letters, close in the Sifaat but not in the points of articulation, situate next to each other. The first letter has Sukoon and the second one has Harakah.

Examples: الذال & الجيم

إِذْ جَاؤُكُمْ

b) The Great Closeness الْمُتَقَارِبَانِ الْكَبِير

Definition: It is when the two letters, close in the Sifaat but not in the points of articulation, situate next to each other. Both of them have Harakah's.

Examples: القاف & الدال

قَدَرٍ مَعْلُومٍ

Relationships Between Letters

c) Mutlaq Closeness الْمُتَقَارِبَانِ الْمُطْلَق

Definition: It is when the two letters, close in the Sifaat but not in the points of articulation, situate next to each other. The first letter has Harakah and the second one has Sukoon.

Examples: القاف & الطاء

يَلْتَقِطْهُ

Ruling: Izhaar in all cases except for the small closeness in some cases as follows:

The Letters	Examples	The Ruling
The Noon Saakin or Tanween followed by the letters ياء - ميم - واو - لام - راء	إِن يَقُولُونَ إِلَّا كَذِبًا سُورَةُ الْكَهْف الآية ٥	Incomplete Idghaam
	فَقَالُواْ رَبَّنَآ ءَاتِنَا مِن لَّدُنكَ رَحْمَةً وَهَيِّئْ لَنَا مِنْ أَمْرِنَا رَشَدًا سُورَةُ الْكَهْف الآية ١٠	Complete Idghaam Incomplete Idghaam
	فَلْيَأْتِكُم بِرِزْقٍ مِّنْهُ سُورَةُ الْكَهْف الآية ١٩	Complete Idghaam
	سَيَقُولُونَ ثَلَثَةٌ رَّابِعُهُمْ كَلْبُهُمْ سُورَةُ الْكَهْف الآية ٢٢ **Exception:** وَقِيلَ مَنْ رَاقٍ سُورَةُ الْقِيَامَة الآية ٢٧	Complete Idghaam Sakt prevents the Complete Idghaam

23

Relationships Between Letters

The letters	Examples	The Ruling
The Noon Saakin or Tanween followed by the Ikhfaa letters except ق - ك	لِمَن شَآءَ مِنكُمْ أَن يَتَقَدَّمَ أَوْ يَتَأَخَّرَ سُورَةُ المُدَّثِّر الآية ﴿٣٧﴾	Ikhfaa
The Noon Saakin or Tanween followed by باء	كَلَّا لَيُنۢبَذَنَّ فِى الْحُطَمَةِ سُورَةُ الهُمَزة الآية ﴿٤﴾	Iqlaab
لام & راء	بَل رَّفَعَهُ اللَّهُ إِلَيْهِ سُورَةُ النِّسَاء الآية ﴿١٥٨﴾	Complete Idghaam
	وَقُل رَّبِّ أَنزِلْنِى مُنزَلاً مُّبَارَكًا سُورَةُ المُؤْمِنُون الآية ﴿٢٩﴾	Complete Idghaam
	Exception: كَلَّا بَلْ رَانَ عَلَىٰ قُلُوبِهِم مَّا كَانُوا۟ يَكْسِبُونَ سُورَةُ المُطَفِّفين الآية ﴿١٤﴾	Sakt prevents the Complete Idghaam
The definite article (ال) and the sun letters	وَجُمِعَ الشَّمْسُ وَالْقَمَرُ سُورَةُ القِيَامَة الآية ﴿٩﴾ فَجَعَلَ مِنْهُ الزَّوْجَيْنِ الذَّكَرَ وَالْأُنثَىٰ سُورَةُ القِيَامَة الآية ﴿٣٩﴾	Complete Idghaam
قاف & كاف	أَلَمْ نَخْلُقكُّم مِّن مَّآءٍ مَّهِينٍ سُورَةُ المُرسَلات الآية ﴿٢٠﴾	Either complete Idghaam or incomplete idghaam by keeping the heaviness of the قاف while pronouncing the كاف

Common mistakes:

The reciter should be careful when pronouncing the following words as most of the beginners make Idghaam:

اَضْطُرَّ - أَفَضْتُمْ - أَوَعَظْتَ

D) The Relationship of Distance - التَّبَاعُد

Definition: It is the relationship between two letters that have distant points of articulation and different characteristics (Sifaat).

There are three types of distant letters:
i) The small distant letters المُتَبَاعِدَانِ الصَغِير
ii) The great distant letters المُتَبَاعِدَانِ الكَبِير
iii) The Mutlaq distant letters المُتَبَاعِدَانِ المُطْلَق

i) The Small Distant Letters المُتَبَاعِدَانِ الصَغِير

Definition: It is when the two distant letters are next to each other. The first letter has Sukoon and the second has Harakah.

Ruling: Izhaar except when the Noon Saakin is followed by قاف & كاف

Examples:

الْمُنْخَنِقَة - أَنكَالًا - أَنقَضَ

Relationships Between Letters

ii) The Great Distant Letters الْمُتَبَاعِدَانِ الْكَبِير

Definition: It is when the two distant letters are next to each other. Both of them have Harakahs.

Ruling: Izhaar

Example: دِهَاقًا

iii) The Mutlaq Distant Letters الْمُتَبَاعِدَانِ الْمُطْلَق

Definition: It is when the two distant letters are next to each other. The first letter has Harakah and the second has Sukoon.

Ruling: Izhaar

Example: أَنفُسُهُمْ

Exercises

1- What are the four different types of relationships between the letters? Define each of them.

2- Define the following:
  1. The small likeness الْمُتَمَاثِلَانِ الصَّغِير
  2. The great likeness الْمُتَمَاثِلَانِ الْكَبِير
  3. The Mutlaq likeness الْمُتَمَاثِلَانِ الْمُطْلَق
  4. The small similarity الْمُتَجَانِسَانِ الصَّغِير
  5. The great similarity الْمُتَجَانِسَانِ الْكَبِير

Exercises

6. The Mutlaq similarity المُتَجَانِسَان المُطْلَق
7. The small distant letters المُتَبَاعِدَان الصَّغِير
8. The great distant letters المُتَبَاعِدَان الكَبِير
9. The Mutlaq distant letters المُتَبَاعِدَان المُطْلَق

3- What are the three categories of the relationship of closeness التَّقَارُب - ?

4- Identify the relationship shared between the following highlighted letters and state the ruling:

1. أَنِ ٱضْرِب بِّعَصَاكَ ٱلْحَجَرَ
2. وَيَجْعَل لَّكَ قُصُورًا
3. إِنَّ ٱلَّذِينَ ءَامَنُواْ وَعَمِلُواْ ٱلصَّٰلِحَٰتِ
4. ذَٰلِكَ بِمَا عَصَواْ وَّكَانُواْ يَعْتَدُونَ
5. مَا سَلَكَكُمْ فِى سَقَرَ
6. قَالُواْ يَٰأَبَانَا مَالَكَ لَا تَأْمَنَّا عَلَىٰ يُوسُفَ
7. شَقَقْنَا
8. فَلَمَّآ أَثْقَلَت دَّعَوَا ٱللَّهَ رَبَّهُمَ
9. قَالَ تَٱللَّهِ إِن كِدتَّ لَتُرْدِينِ
10. إِذْ هَمَّت طَّآئِفَتَانِ مِنكُمْ
11. عَلَىٰ مَا فَرَّطتُ فِى جَنۢبِ ٱللَّهِ
12. وَلَوْ أَنَّهُمْ إِذ ظَّلَمُوٓاْ أَنفُسَهُمْ

13. يَلْهَث ذَّٰلِكَ
14. ٱلصَّٰلِحَٰتِ طُوبَىٰ
15. أَفَتَطْمَعُونَ
16. أَفَضْتُمْ
17. كَذَّبَتْ ثَمُودُ
18. مِن فَوْقِكُمْ
19. وَلَا يَسْتَثْنُونَ
20. عَدَدَ سِنِينَ
21. إِذْ جَاؤُكُمْ
22. يَلْتَقِطْهُ
23. مِن لَّدُنكَ رَحْمَةً وَهَيِّئْ
24. وَقِيلَ مَنْ رَاقٍ
25. لِمَن شَآءَ مِنكُمْ

Third Section

The Rules
of Two Saakin Letters
Meeting Together

حُكْمُ الْتِقَاءِ السَّاكِنَيْنِ

Jannat
Al Quran

The Rules of Two Saakin Letters Meeting Together حُكْمُ الْتِقَاءِ السَّاكِنَيْنِ

This could occur in one word or between two words.

A) The Rules of Two Saakin Letters Meeting Together in One Word

In case of stopping:

The two Saakin letters will meet in case of stopping only.

1- The first Saakin is a letter of Madd

Examples: الْعَالَمِينَ - الْأَبْرَارَ

Ruling: The reciter can prolong the Madd letter 2 or 4 or 6 Harakas. When joining these words to the next word, natural Madd is pronounced.

2- The first Saakin is a letter of Leen

Examples: بَيْتٍ - خَوْفٍ

Ruling: The reciter can prolong the Leen letter 2 or 4 or 6 Harakas. When joining these words to the next word, the letter of Leen is pronounced.

3- The first Saakin is neither a letter of Madd nor a letter of Leen

Examples: الْفَجْرِ - الْأَرْضُ

Ruling: The Saakin letter will be pronounced the same way as when continuing recitation.

The Rules of Two Saakin Letters Meeting Together حُكْمُ الْتِقَاءِ السَّاكِنَيْنِ

In case of stopping and continuing recitation:

The two Saakin letters will meet in case of stopping and continuing recitation.

Examples: الْحَاقَّة - ءَآلْـٰٔنَ - الٓمٓ

Ruling: The letter of Madd is prolonged 6 Harakas.

B) The Rules of Two Saakin Letters Meeting Together in Two Words.

1- A word ending with a Madd letter precedes a word which starts with a Sukoon.

Examples: وَعَمِلُوا الصَّالِحاتِ - وَقَالَـا الْحَمْدُ - فِى السَّمَاءِ

Ruling:

i) When stopping on the first word, the letter of Madd is pronounced.

ii) When joining the two words, the Madd letter is dropped in order to avoid the meeting of two Saakins.

2- A word ending with Tanween precedes a word which starts with a Sukoon.

Examples: خَيْرًا الْوَصِيَّةُ - لَهُوًا انفَضُّوٓا - يَوْمَئِذٍ ٱلْمَسَاقُ

Ruling: The Tanween will be pronounced with Kasrah.

The Rules of Two Saakin Letters Meeting Together حُكْمُ الْتِقَاءِ السَّاكِنَيْنِ

Note: الٓمٓ at the beginning of Surah Al-Imran has a special rule as الٓمٓ is followed by Saakin.

الٓمٓ ۝ اللَّهُ لَآ إِلَٰهَ إِلَّا هُوَ ٱلْحَىُّ ٱلْقَيُّومُ ۝

When joining الٓمٓ to ٱللَّهُ, two Saakin letters will meet; Meem Saakin and Laam Saakin. To avoid this meeting, two pronunciations for الٓمٓ are possible.

i) Meem is prolonged to 2 Harakas and is pronounced with Fathah.

ii) Meem is prolonged to 6 Harakas and is pronounced with Fathah.

Exercises

1- What are the rules of the meeting of two Saakin letters when stopping on the following words:

1- الْأَبْرَارَ

2- بَيْتٍ

3- الْفَجْرِ

4- ءَآلْـٰٔنَ

5- فِى السَّمَاءِ

2- What are the rules of joining الٓمٓ to ٱللَّه in Surah Al-Imran.

Fourth Section

The Possessive Pronoun

هَاءُ الْكِنَايَة

Jannat
Al Quran

The Possessive Pronoun
هَاءُ الْكِنَايَة

Definition:

It is the possessive pronoun هاء that indicates a singular male in the third person. This هاء is extra and not part of the original makeup of the word. Further, it is always found at the end of words.

The possessive pronoun هَاءُ الْكِنَايَة will have Dhammah unless it is preceded by a letter that has Kasrah or ياء. In these cases it will be pronounced with a Kasrah.

There are four different positions of the possessive pronoun within a word.

1- The possessive pronoun is situated between two letters that have Harakas.
Examples:

وَلَمْ يَكُن لَّهُۥ كُفُوًا أَحَدُۢ   سُورَةُ الْإِخْلَاص الآية ④

إِنَّهُۥ كَانَ تَوَّابًۢا   سُورَةُ النَّصْر الآية ③

مَا لَهُم بِهِۦ مِنْ عِلْمٍ إِلَّا ٱتِّبَاعَ ٱلظَّنِّ   سُورَةُ النِّسَاء الآية ⑰

إِنَّهُۥ كَانَ بِعِبَادِهِۦ خَبِيرًۢا بَصِيرًا   سُورَةُ الْإِسْرَاء الآية ③

قَالَ لَهُۥ صَاحِبُهُۥ وَهُوَ يُحَاوِرُهُۥ أَكَفَرْتَ بِٱلَّذِى خَلَقَكَ مِن تُرَابٍ سُورَةُ الْكَهْف الآية ③

فَتَمَّ مِيقَـٰتُ رَبِّهِۦ أَرْبَعِينَ لَيْلَةً   سُورَةُ الْأَعْرَاف الآية ⑭

31

The Possessive Pronoun
هَاءُ الْكِنَايَة

Rulings:

i) The possessive pronoun هَاءُ الْكِنَايَة will be prolonged to 2 Harakas when it is followed by any letter other than Hamza. This is called The Small Connective Lengthening.

The sign in Quran: A small Waaw و when the هاء is preceded by a letter that has a Dhammah.

A small Yaa ـ when the هاء is preceded by a letter that has a Kasrah.

ii) The possessive pronoun هَاءُ الْكِنَايَة will be prolonged to 4 Harakas when it is followed by a Hamza. This is called The Great Connective Lengthening.

The sign in Quran: A small Waaw and a Madd sign و when the هاء is preceded by a letter that has a Dhammah.

A small Yaa and a Madd sign ـ when the هاء is preceded by a letter that has a Kasrah.

Example:

سُورَةُ الْأَعْرَاف الآية ٧٣ هَـٰذِهِۦ نَاقَةُ ٱللَّهِ لَكُمْ ءَايَةً

If the هاء of هذه, which indicates a singular female, is situated between two letters that have Harakas, the small ياء will be prolonged to 2 Harakas.

The Possessive Pronoun
هَاءُ الْكِنَايَة

Exceptions:

1- وَمَآ أَنسَنِيهُ إِلَّا ٱلشَّيْطَنُ أَنْ أَذْكُرَهُ سُورَةُ الْكَهْفِ الْآيَةِ ۶۳

The possessive pronoun هَاءُ الْكِنَايَة is pronounced with Dhammah although it is preceded with ياء.

2- وَمَنْ أَوْفَى بِمَا عَهَدَ عَلَيْهُ ٱللَّهَ فَسَيُؤْتِيهِ أَجْرًا عَظِيمًا سُورَةُ الْفَتْحِ الْآيَةِ ۱۰

The possessive pronoun هَاءُ الْكِنَايَة is pronounced with Dhammah although it is preceded with ياء.

3- قَالُوٓا أَرْجِهْ وَأَخَاهُ وَأَرْسِلْ فِى ٱلْمَدَآئِنِ حَشِرِينَ سُورَةُ الْأَعْرَافِ الْآيَةِ ۱۱۱

The possessive pronoun هَاءُ الْكِنَايَة is not prolonged.

4- اذْهَب بِّكِتَٰبِى هَٰذَا فَأَلْقِهْ إِلَيْهِمْ سُورَةُ النَّمْلِ الْآيَةِ ۲۸

The possessive pronoun هَاءُ الْكِنَايَة is not prolonged.

5- وَإِن تَشْكُرُوا۟ يَرْضَهُ لَكُمْ سُورَةُ الزُّمَرِ الْآيَةِ ۷

The possessive pronoun هَاءُ الْكِنَايَة is not prolonged.

The Possessive Pronoun

هَاءُ الْكِنَايَة

2- The possessive pronoun is situated between two letters that both have Sukoon

Example:

شَهْرُ رَمَضَانَ ٱلَّذِىٓ أُنزِلَ فِيهِ ٱلْقُرْءَانُ   سُورَةُ الْبَقَرَة الآية (١٨٥)

Ruling: **The possessive pronoun** هَاءُ الْكِنَايَة **is not prolonged.**

3- The possessive pronoun is preceded by a letter that has Harakah and followed by a letter that has Sukoon

Example:

تَبَـٰرَكَ ٱلَّذِى بِيَدِهِ ٱلْمُلْكُ وَهُوَ عَلَىٰ كُلِّ شَىْءٍ قَدِيرٌ   سُورَةُ الْمُلْك الآية (١)

Ruling: **The possessive pronoun** هَاءُ الْكِنَايَة **is not prolonged.**

4- The possessive pronoun is preceded by a letter that has Sukoon and followed by a letter that has Harakah

Example:

ذَٰلِكَ ٱلْكِتَـٰبُ لَا رَيْبَ فِيهِ هُدًى لِّلْمُتَّقِينَ   سُورَةُ الْبَقَرَة الآية (٢)

Ruling: **The possessive pronoun** هَاءُ الْكِنَايَة **will not be prolonged.**

Exception: وَيَخْلُدْ فِيهِۦ مُهَانًا   سُورَةُ الْفُرْقَان الآية (٦٩)

The possessive pronoun هَاءُ الْكِنَايَة **is prolonged.**

Exercises

1- What is the definition of the possessive pronoun هَاءُ الْكِنَايَة؟

2- What are the different positions of the possessive pronoun within a word? Give examples.

Fifth Section

The Silent & Pronounced Alif

Jannat
Al Quran

There are seven Alifs in the Quran that come at the end of some words. They are pronounced when stopping and dropped when continuing. These Alifs have on oval shaped Sukoon on top of them "0"

1- وَلَا أَنَا۠ عَابِدٌ مَّا عَبَدتُّمْ سُورَةُ الْكَافِرُون الآية ﴿٤﴾

Note: أنا occurred many times in the Quran.

2- لَٰكِنَّا هُوَ ٱللَّهُ رَبِّي وَلَآ أُشْرِكُ بِرَبِّيٓ أَحَدًا سُورَةُ الْكَهْف الآية ﴿٣٨﴾

3- وَإِذْ زَاغَتِ ٱلْأَبْصَٰرُ وَبَلَغَتِ ٱلْقُلُوبُ ٱلْحَنَاجِرَ وَتَظُنُّونَ بِٱللَّهِ ٱلظُّنُونَا۠
سُورَةُ الْأَحْزَاب الآية ﴿١٠﴾

4- يَوْمَ تُقَلَّبُ وُجُوهُهُمْ فِي ٱلنَّارِ يَقُولُونَ يَٰلَيْتَنَآ أَطَعْنَا ٱللَّهَ وَأَطَعْنَا
ٱلرَّسُولَا۠ سُورَةُ الْأَحْزَاب الآية ﴿٦٦﴾

5- وَقَالُوا۟ رَبَّنَآ إِنَّآ أَطَعْنَا سَادَتَنَا وَكُبَرَآءَنَا فَأَضَلُّونَا ٱلسَّبِيلَا۠
سُورَةُ الْأَحْزَاب الآية ﴿٦٧﴾

6- وَيُطَافُ عَلَيْهِم بِـَٔانِيَةٍ مِّن فِضَّةٍ وَأَكْوَابٍ كَانَتْ قَوَارِيرَا۠
سُورَةُ الْإِنْسَان الآية ﴿١٥﴾

7- إِنَّآ أَعْتَدْنَا لِلْكَٰفِرِينَ سَلَٰسِلَا۠ وَأَغْلَٰلًا وَسَعِيرًا
سُورَةُ الْإِنْسَان الآية ﴿٤﴾

The Silent & Pronounced Alif

When stopping on سَلَسِلَا۟, two pronunciations are possible.

1- Dropping the Alif and pronouncing the Laam with a Sukoon.

2- The Alif is pronounced.

When joining سَلَسِلَا۟ to the next word, the Alif is dropped.

Note: There is an Alif that has "o". This Alif is not pronounced when stopping on the word nor when continuing the recitation.

Example:

إِنَّ ٱلَّذِينَ ءَامَنُواْ وَعَمِلُواْ ٱلصَّـٰلِحَـٰتِ أُوْلَـٰٓئِكَ هُمْ خَيْرُ ٱلْبَرِيَّةِ

سُورَةُ الْبَيِّنَة الآية ۷

37

Sixth Section

Stopping
and Starting Recitation

الْوَقْفُ وَالْإِبْتِدَاء

Jannat
Al Quran

Stopping and Starting Recitation
الْوَقْفُ وَالْإِبْتِدَاء

It is impossible for the reciter to recite any Surah in one breath; therefore, it is essential that the reciter learns the appropriate positions where they could stop their recitation, and where they could resume it.

Definition: Cutting off the sound at the end of a word in the Quran for a limited period for breathing, with the intention of resuming recitation. Stopping is permissible at the end or in the middle of an Ayah, but it is not permissible in the middle of a word.

There are four types of stops:
a) The Compelled Stop - الْوَقْفُ الْإِضْرَارِي
b) The Test Stop - الْوَقْفُ الْإِخْتِبَارِي
c) The Comprehensive Stop - الْوَقْفُ الْإِنْتِظَارِي
d) The Optional Stop - الْوَقْفُ الْإِخْتِيَارِي

A) The Compelled Stop - الْوَقْفُ الْإِضْرَارِي

Definition: This is the cutting of the sound at the end of a word in the Quran for a compelled reason such as shortness of breath, crying, sneezing or coughing. This may prevent the reciter from stopping on a word that conveys a sound or complete meaning.

Stopping and Starting Recitation
الْوَقْفُ وَالْإِبْتِدَاء

Ruling: It is permissible for the reciter to stop at the end of any word in the Quran for a compelled reason, even if the meaning is not complete. However, they must resume the recitation from a word that conveys a sound and complete meaning. This may require that the reciter repeats some words to achieve that.

B) The Test Stop - الْوَقْفُ الْإِخْتِبَارِي

Definition: This is when a student is asked to stop when being tested by the teacher.

Ruling: It is permissible for the reciter to stop on any word in the Quran when being examined for their knowledge of Tajweed rules, even if the meaning is not complete. However, they must resume the recitation from a word that conveys a sound and complete meaning. This may require that the reciter repeats some words to achieve that.

Example:

وَجَعَلْنَـٰهَا رُجُومًا لِّلشَّيَـٰطِينِّ

The teacher may ask the student to stop on the word رُجُومًا to test them on the rule of Tajweed.

Stopping and Starting Recitation
الْوَقْفُ وَالْإِبْتِدَاء

C) The Comprehensive Stop - الْوَقْفُ الْإِنْتِظَارِي

Definition: This is stopping the recitation on a word which has more than one way of reciting, to apply a ruling related to a particular word and recite the certain ways of pronunciation of this word.

Ruling: It is permissible for the reciter to stop on any word in the Quran to apply a ruling related to a certain word and recite the certain ways of pronunciation of this word. However, they must resume the recitation from a word that conveys a sound and complete meaning. This may require the reciter to repeat some words..

Example: أَلَمْ نَخْلُقكُّم مِّن مَّآءٍ مَّهِينٍ سُورَةُ الْمُرسَلات الآية۞

D) The Optional Stop - الْوَقْفُ الْإِخْتِيَارِي

Definition: It is a decision made by the reciter to stop at the end of a word. The reciter must choose to stop on a word that conveys a sound meaning.

There are four types of the optional stop الْوَقْفُ الْإِخْتِيَارِي:

1- The Complete Stop الْوَقْفُ التَّام
2- The Sufficient Stop الْوَقْفُ الْكَافِي
3- The Good Stop الْوَقْفُ الْحَسَن
4- The Repulsive Stop الْوَقْفُ الْقَبِيح

Stopping and Starting Recitation
الْوَقْفُ وَالْإِبْتِدَاء

1- The Complete Stop الْوَقْفُ التَّام

Definition: It is stopping at the end of a word that conveys a sound and complete meaning and is not attached to what follows in meaning or in grammatical expression.

The Complete Stop الْوَقْفُ التَّام occurs in the following cases:

1- At the end of an Ayah.

2- After the completion of a subject such as speaking about the heaven and the hell.

3- After the completion of a story such as the story of prophet Musa (pbup).

4- At the end of a word within an Ayah where the word conveys a sound and complete meaning and is not attached to what follows in meaning or in grammar.

Ruling: It is preferable for the reciter to stop at this position as it gives a good meaning, and it is permissible to resume the recitation from what follows without the need to repeat some words.

Examples:

1- At the end of an Ayah.

مَـٰلِكِ يَوْمِ ٱلدِّينِ (4) إِيَّاكَ نَعْبُدُ وَإِيَّاكَ نَسْتَعِينُ (5)

The Master of the Day of Requital. (4) You alone do we worship, and from You alone do we seek help. (5)

سُورَةُ الْفَاتِحَة الآية ٤ ٥

Stopping and Starting Recitation
الْوَقْفُ وَالْإِبْتِدَاء

2- After the completion of a subject

أُوْلَـٰٓئِكَ عَلَىٰ هُدًى مِّن رَّبِّهِمْ ۖ وَأُوْلَـٰٓئِكَ هُمُ ٱلْمُفْلِحُونَ (5) إِنَّ ٱلَّذِينَ كَفَرُوا۟ سَوَآءٌ عَلَيْهِمْ ءَأَنذَرْتَهُمْ أَمْ لَمْ تُنذِرْهُمْ لَا يُؤْمِنُونَ (6)

They are on (true) guidance from their Lord, and they are the successful. (5) Verily, those who disbelieve, it is the same to them whether you (O Muhammad Peace be upon him) warn them or do not warn them, they will not believe. (6)

سُورَةُ الْبَقَرَة الآية ٦

3- After the completion of a story

تِلْكَ مِنْ أَنۢبَآءِ ٱلْغَيْبِ نُوحِيهَآ إِلَيْكَ ۖ مَا كُنتَ تَعْلَمُهَآ أَنتَ وَلَا قَوْمُكَ مِن قَبْلِ هَـٰذَا ۖ فَٱصْبِرْ ۖ إِنَّ ٱلْعَـٰقِبَةَ لِلْمُتَّقِينَ (49) وَإِلَىٰ عَادٍ أَخَاهُمْ هُودًا ۚ قَالَ يَـٰقَوْمِ ٱعْبُدُوا۟ ٱللَّهَ مَا لَكُم مِّنْ إِلَـٰهٍ غَيْرُهُۥٓ ۖ إِنْ أَنتُمْ إِلَّا مُفْتَرُونَ (50)

This is of the news of the unseen which We reveal unto you (O Muhammad SAW), neither you nor your people knew it before this. So be patient. Surely, the (good) end is for the Al-Muttaqûn (pious) (49) And to 'Ad (people We sent) their brother Hûd. He said, "O my people! Worship Allâh! You have no other ilâh (god) but Him. Certainly, you do nothing but invent lies! (50)

سُورَةُ هُود الآية ٤٩ ٥٠

42

Stopping and Starting Recitation

الْوَقْفُ وَالْإِبْتِدَاء

4- At the end of a word within an Ayah where the word conveys a sound and complete meaning and is not attached to what follows in meaning or in grammatical expression.

لَقَدْ أَضَلَّنِي عَنِ ٱلذِّكْرِ بَعْدَ إِذْ جَآءَنِي ۗ وَكَانَ ٱلشَّيْطَـٰنُ لِلْإِنسَـٰنِ خَذُولاً (29)

"He indeed led me astray from the Reminder (this Qur'ân) after it had come to me. And Shaitân (Satan) is to man ever a deserter in the hour of need." (29)

سُورَةُ الْفُرْقَان الآية ٢٩

The first part of the Ayah is the words of the disbelievers whereas the second part is the words of Allah.

The sign in the Quran is ۗ
which means the preference is to stop الْوَقْفُ أَوْلَى

Note: There is a specific type of complete stop الْوَقْفُ التَّام where it is compulsory to stop. This type of stopping is called Compulsory Stop الْوَقْفُ اللاَّزِم.

Definition: It is stopping at the end of a word that conveys a sound and complete meaning and is not attached to what follows in meaning or grammatically. If the reciter doesn't stop on this word, the listener will misinterpret the Ayah as the meaning conveyed to him is repulsive.

Stopping and Starting Recitation
الْوَقْفُ وَالْإِبْتِدَاء

Ruling: It is compulsory to stop on this word.
The sign in the Quran is مـ

Examples: (65) وَلَا يَحْزُنكَ قَوْلُهُمْ إِنَّ ٱلْعِزَّةَ لِلَّهِ جَمِيعًا هُوَ ٱلسَّمِيعُ ٱلْعَلِيمُ
And let not their speech grieve you (O Muhammad SAW), for all power and honour belong to Allâh. He is the All-Hearer, the All-Knower. سُورَةُ يُونُس ۝
In the first part of the Ayah, Allah addresses Prophet Muhammad (SAW) and tells him not to grieve because of what the disbelievers were saying. On the other hand, the second part speaks of Allah's might and honour. If the reader doesn't stop, the listener may think that the disbelievers say, "for all power and honour belong to Allâh", which is a wrong meaning.

2- The Sufficient Stop الْوَقْفُ الْكَافِي
Definition: It is stopping at the end of a word that conveys a sound and complete meaning, and is attached to what follows in meaning but not grammatically.
The complete stop الْوَقْفُ الْكَافِي occurs in the following cases:
1- At the end of an Ayah.
2- At the end of a word within an Ayah, where the word conveys a sound and a complete meaning and is attached to what follows grammatically.

Stopping and Starting Recitation
الْوَقْفُ وَالْإِبْتِدَاء

Ruling: It is permissible for the reciter to stop at this position as it gives a good meaning. It is also permissible to resume the recitation from what follows without the need to repeat some words.

Examples:

1- At the end of an Ayah

ٱلَّذِينَ يُؤْمِنُونَ بِٱلْغَيْبِ وَيُقِيمُونَ ٱلصَّلَوٰةَ وَمِمَّا رَزَقْنَـٰهُمْ يُنفِقُونَ (3) وَٱلَّذِينَ يُؤْمِنُونَ بِمَآ أُنزِلَ إِلَيْكَ وَمَآ أُنزِلَ مِن قَبْلِكَ وَبِٱلْأَخِرَةِ هُمْ يُوقِنُونَ (4)

Who believe in the Ghaib[] and perform As-Salât (Iqâmat-as-Salât), and spend out of what we have provided for them [i.e. give Zakât, spend on themselves, their parents, their children, their wives, etc., and also give charity to the poor and also in Allâh's Cause - Jihâd,]. (3) And who believe in (the Qurân and the Sunnah)[] which has been sent down (revealed) to you (Muhammad Peace be upon him) and in that which we sent down before [the Taurât (Torah) and the Injeel (Gospel), etc.] and they believe with certainty in the Hereafter. (Resurrection, recompense of their good and bad deeds, Paradise and Hell,) (4)

سُورَةُ الْبَقَرَة الآية (٣) ﴿٤﴾

These two Ayahs are linked in meaning but not grammatically.

Stopping and Starting Recitation
الْوَقْفُ وَالْإِبْتِدَاء

2- At the end of a word within an Ayah where the word conveys a sound and complete meaning but is not attached to what follows grammatically

أَمْ حَسِبْتُمْ أَن تَدْخُلُواْ ٱلْجَنَّةَ وَلَمَّا يَأْتِكُم مَّثَلُ ٱلَّذِينَ خَلَوْاْ مِن قَبْلِكُم مَّسَّتْهُمُ ٱلْبَأْسَآءُ وَٱلضَّرَّآءُ وَزُلْزِلُواْ حَتَّىٰ يَقُولَ ٱلرَّسُولُ وَٱلَّذِينَ ءَامَنُواْ مَعَهُۥ مَتَىٰ نَصْرُ ٱللَّهِ أَلَآ إِنَّ نَصْرَ ٱللَّهِ قَرِيبٌ (214)

Or think you that you will enter Paradise without such (trials) as came to those who passed away before you? They were afflicted with severe poverty and ailments and were so shaken that even the Messenger and those who believed along with him said, "When (will come) the Help of Allâh?" Yes! Certainly, the Help of Allâh is near! (214)

سُورَةُ الْبَقَرَةِ الْآية ۲۱٤

The first part of the Ayah is linked to the second part in the meaning but not in the grammatical rules.

The sign in the Quran is ج صلى -

صلى means the preference is to continue الْوَصْلُ أَوْلَى

ج means the reciter has the choice to either stop or continue جَوَازُ الْوَقْف

46

Stopping and Starting Recitation
الْوَقْفُ وَالْإِبْتِدَاء

3- The Good Stop الْوَقْفُ الْحَسَن
Definition: It is stopping at the end of a word that conveys a sound meaning, and is linked to what follows both in meaning and in grammar.

The Good Stop الْوَقْفُ الْحَسَن occurs in the following cases:

1- At the end of an Ayah. Note that it is Sunnah to stop at the end of each Ayah.

2- At the end of a word within an Ayah where the word is attached to what follows in meaning and in grammar but the meaning is not repulsive.

Ruling: It is permissible for the reciter to stop on any word in the Quran as long as the meaning is not repulsive. However, they must resume the recitation from a word that conveys a sound and complete meaning. This may require that the reciter repeats some words.

Examples:

بِسْمِ اللهِ الرَّحْمَـٰنِ الرَّحِيمِ (1

In the name of Allah, the Beneficent, the Merciful (1)

سُوْرَةُ الْفَاتِحَة الآية①

الْحَمْدُ للهِ رَبِّ الْعَـٰلَمِينَ (2

All the praises and thanks be to Allah, the Lord of the 'Âlamîn (mankind, jinn and all that exists). (2)

سُوْرَةُ الْفَاتِحَة الآية②

47

Stopping and Starting Recitation
الْوَقْفُ وَالْإِبْتِدَاء

Note:
Sometimes the end of Ayah doesn't covey a complete meaning and may be misinterpreted.

Example:

فَوَيْلٌ لِّلْمُصَلِّينَ (4) ٱلَّذِينَ هُمْ عَن صَلَاتِهِمْ سَاهُونَ (5)
So woe unto those performers of Salât (prayers) (hypocrites), (4) Those who delay their Salât (prayer from their stated fixed times), (5)
سُورَةُ الْمَاعُون الآية ۝ ۝

There are three opinions for the scholars:
1- It is not permissible to stop.
2- It is permissible to stop for a limited period for breathing with the intention of resuming recitation as stopping at the end of an Ayah is Sunnah.
3- It is permissible to stop. However, the reciter should repeat this Ayah and join it with the next one.

4- The Repulsive Stop الْوَقْفُ الْقَبِيح

Definition: It is stopping at the end of a word that does not convey a complete and sound meaning as it is strongly linked to what follows it in the meaning and the grammatical rules.

Stopping and Starting Recitation

الْوَقْفُ وَالْإِبْتِدَاء

The Repulsive Stop الْوَقْفُ الْقَبِيح occurs in the following cases within an Ayah:

1- Stopping on a word that conveys an incomplete meaning.

2- Stopping on a word that conveys a meaning that is in contrast to what is intended.

3- Stopping on a word that conveys a meaning that is inappropriate to Allah (SWT).

Ruling: It is not permissible for the reciter to stop on a word in the Quran if the meaning is repulsive. It is considered a sin if the reciter intentionally applies a repulsive stop, but not a sin if done by mistake. However, the reciter must resume the recitation from a word that conveys a sound and complete meaning. This may necessitate the reciter to repeat some words.

Examples:

1- Stopping on a word that conveys an incomplete meaning

بِسْمِ ٱللهِ ٱلرَّحْمَـٰنِ ٱلرَّحِيمِ

In the name of Allah, the Beneficent, the Merciful (1)

سُورَةُ الْفَاتِحَة الآية①

Stopping and Starting Recitation
الْوَقْفُ وَالْإِبْتِدَاء

2- Stopping on a word that conveys a meaning that is in contrast to what is intended

يَـٰٓأَيُّهَا ٱلَّذِينَ ءَامَنُواْ لَا تَقْرَبُواْ ٱلصَّلَوٰةَ وَأَنتُمْ سُكَـٰرَىٰ حَتَّىٰ تَعْلَمُواْ مَا تَقُولُونَ وَلَا جُنُبًا إِلَّا عَابِرِى سَبِيلٍ حَتَّىٰ تَغْتَسِلُواْ

O you who believe! Approach not As-Salât (the prayer) when you are in a drunken state until you know (the meaning) of what you utter, nor when you are in a state of Janâba, (i.e. in a state of sexual impurity and have not yet taken a bath) except when travelling on the road (without enough water, or just passing through a mosque), till you wash your whole body.

سُورَةُ النِّسَاء الآية ٤٣

3- Stopping on a word that conveys a meaning that is inappropriate to Allah (SWT)

فَبُهِتَ ٱلَّذِى كَفَرَّ وَٱللَّهُ لَا يَهْدِى ٱلْقَوْمَ ٱلظَّـٰلِمِينَ

So the disbeliever was utterly defeated. And Allâh guides not the people, who are Zâlimûn (wrong-doers).

سُورَةُ الْبَقَرَة الآية ٢٥٨

50

Stopping and Starting Recitation
الْوَقْفُ وَالْإِبْتِدَاء

Pausing السَّكْت

Definition: Cutting off the sound at the end of a word in the Quran for a period less than that of stopping without breathing, and with the intention of resuming recitation.

The sign in the Quran is س

There are four required pauses in the Quran:

ٱلْحَمْدُ لِلّٰهِ ٱلَّذِىٓ أَنزَلَ عَلَىٰ عَبْدِهِ ٱلْكِتَٰبَ وَلَمْ يَجْعَل لَّهُۥ عِوَجَاۜ (1) قَيِّمًا

لِّيُنذِرَ بَأْسًا شَدِيدًا مِّن لَّدُنْهُ وَيُبَشِّرَ ٱلْمُؤْمِنِينَ ٱلَّذِينَ يَعْمَلُونَ

ٱلصَّٰلِحَٰتِ أَنَّ لَهُمْ أَجْرًا حَسَنًا (2) سُورَةُ الْكَهْفِ الآية ١ ۝

قَالُواْ يَٰوَيْلَنَا مَنۢ بَعَثَنَا مِن مَّرْقَدِنَاۜ هَٰذَا مَا وَعَدَ ٱلرَّحْمَٰنُ وَصَدَقَ

ٱلْمُرْسَلُونَ   سُورَةُ س الآية ٥٢ ۝

وَقِيلَ مَنْۜ رَاقٍ   سُورَةُ الْقِيَامَة الآية ٢٧ ۝

كَلَّاۜ بَلْۜ رَانَ عَلَىٰ قُلُوبِهِم مَّا كَانُواْ يَكْسِبُونَ   سُورَةُ الْمُطَفِّفِين الآية ١٤ ۝

Ruling: It is obligatory for the reciter to pause.

51

Stopping and Starting Recitation
الْوَقْفُ وَالْإِبْتِدَاء

There are two permitted pauses:

1- At the end Surah Al-Anfal when joining it to the beginning of Surah At-Tawbah.

إِنَّ ٱللَّهَ بِكُلِّ شَىْءٍ عَلِيمٌ (75) بَرَآءَةٌ مِّنَ ٱللَّهِ وَرَسُولِهِۦٓ إِلَى ٱلَّذِينَ عَٰهَدتُّم مِّنَ ٱلْمُشْرِكِينَ (1)

Ruling: When joining the two Ayahs, it is permissible for the reciter to pause or to make Iqlaab.

2- Surah Al-Haqah.

مَآ أَغْنَىٰ عَنِّى مَالِيَهْ (28) هَلَكَ عَنِّى سُلْطَٰنِيَهْ (29)

Ruling: When joining the two Ayahs, it is permissible for the reciter to pause or to make Idghaam. Pausing is preferable.

Terminating الْقَطْع

Definition: Cutting off the sound at the end of a word in the Quran without the intention of resuming the recitation.

Ruling: It is permissible to terminate the recitation at the end of a Surah or an Ayah where stopping is not repulsive, but not in the middle of an Ayah or a word.

Stopping and Starting Recitation
الْوَقْفُ وَالْإِبْتِدَاء

The difference between stopping and pausing:

Stopping	Pausing
The reciter takes his breath	The reciter does not take his breath
The meaning must be complete	The meaning may not be complete
It does not have specific positions in the Quran	It has six specific positions in the Quran
The period of stopping is longer than that of pausing	The period of pausing is shorter than that of stopping

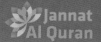

Signs of Stopping

ـمـ	Compulsory stop الْوَقْفُ اللَّازِم The reciter has to stop. Continuation is prohibited
قلى	The preference is to stop الْوَقْفُ أَوْلَى
صلى	The preference is to continue الْوَصْلُ أَوْلَى
ج	The reciter has the choice to either stop or continue جَوَازُ الْوَقْف
∴ ∴	The reciter can stop at either of the points but not both تَعَانُقُ الْوَقْف
لا	It is not permissible to stop.
س	سكت It is obligatory for the reciter to pause
سجدة	The sign 🔲 indicates that there is Sajda which is Sunnah, the sign _____ explains the reason why we have to make Sajda. Sajda occurred 14 times in the Quran: Surah 7:206, Surah 13:15, Surah 16:49, Surah 17:107, Surah 19:58, Surah 22:77, Surah 25:60, Surah 27:25, Surah 32:15, Surah 38:24, Surah 41:37, Surah 53:59, Surah 84:21, Surah 96:19.

Exercises

1- What is the definition of:
stopping, pausing, terminating the recitation?

2- What are are four reasons for stopping? Define each one and mention its ruling.

3- What are the four kinds of the optional stop الْوَقْفُ الْإِخْتِيَارِي ?

Important Notes

1- The Accent النَّبْر

Definition: Pressure on a part or a specific letter of the word, so that it sounds slightly louder than that of the other letters. It is applied when stopping on a word that has a Shaddah on the last letter.

Examples:

وَتُخْرِجُ ٱلْحَىَّ مِنَ ٱلْمَيِّتِ وَتُخْرِجُ ٱلْمَيِّتَ مِنَ ٱلْحَيِّ سُورَةُ آل عِمْرَان الآية ⑳

فَإِن لَّمْ يُصِبْهَا وَابِلٌ فَطَلٌّ سُورَةُ الْبَقَرَة الآية ⑭

2- Imalah إِمَالَة

It occurs once in the Quran. It means that the Alif is pronounced slanted towards the Yaa.

وَقَالَ ٱرْكَبُواْ فِيهَا بِسْمِ ٱللَّهِ مَجْرٜىٰهَا وَمُرْسَىٰهَآ   سُورَةُ هُود الآية ⑪

The sign in Quran is either a black bullet ● or a diamond shape ◆.

3- In two instances, the letter س placed on the top of the letter ص.

This indicates that the letter س should be pronounced instead of the letter ص.

Important Notes

مَن ذَا ٱلَّذِى يُقْرِضُ ٱللَّهَ قَرْضًا حَسَنًا فَيُضَٰعِفَهُۥ لَهُۥ أَضْعَافًا كَثِيرَةً وَٱللَّهُ يَقْبِضُ وَيَبْصُۜطُ وَإِلَيْهِ تُرْجَعُونَ

سُورَةُ ٱلْبَقَرَةِ ٱلآية ﴿٢٤٥﴾

وَٱذْكُرُوٓاْ إِذْ جَعَلَكُمْ خُلَفَآءَ مِنۢ بَعْدِ قَوْمِ نُوحٍ وَزَادَكُمْ فِى ٱلْخَلْقِ بَصْۜطَةً

سُورَةُ ٱلأَعْرَافِ ٱلآية ﴿٦٩﴾

4- In one instance, the letter س placed below the letter ص.

This indicates that the reciter has the choice either to pronounce س or ص.

أَمْ عِندَهُمْ خَزَآئِنُ رَبِّكَ أَمْ هُمُ ٱلْمُصَۜيْطِرُونَ

سُورَةُ ٱلطُّورِ ٱلآية ﴿٣٧﴾

57

Printed in Great Britain
by Amazon

29830527R00041